UKULELE

LA LA LAND

MUSIC FROM THE MOTION PICTURE SOUNDTRACK

ISBN 978-1-4950-8990-9

7777 W. BLUEMOUND RD. P.O. BOX 13819 MILWAUKEE, WI 53213

In Australia Contact:
Hal Leonard Australia Pty. Ltd.
4 Lentara Court
Cheltenham, Victoria, 3192 Australia
Email: ausadmin@halleonard.com.au

Visit Hal Leonard Online at
www.halleonard.com

Another Day of Sun

Music by Justin Hurwitz
Lyrics by Benj Pasek & Justin Paul

lights are down, _ he'll see my face and think of how _ he
come a - long. _____ That - 'll be the thing to push _ him

Chorus

used to know me. }
on and go, go. } Climb these hills, I'm

reach - ing for the heights and chas - ing all the

lights that shine. ____
(The lights that when shine.) ____ And when they

let you down, _ you get up
(It's an - oth - er day of...)

off the ground. _ The morn - in'
(It's an - oth - er day of...)

4

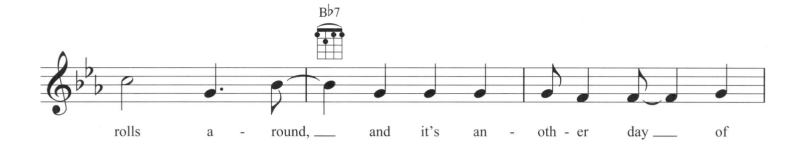

rolls   a - round, ___   and   it's   an - oth - er   day ___   of

To Coda ⊕

D.S. al Coda
(take 2nd ending)

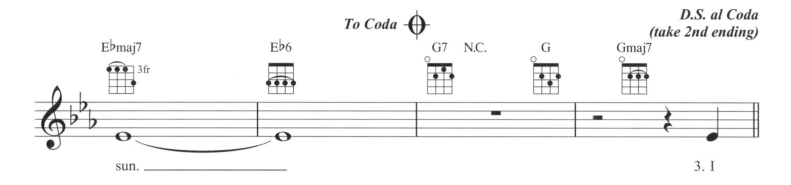

sun. _____

3. I

⊕ **Coda**

Instrumental

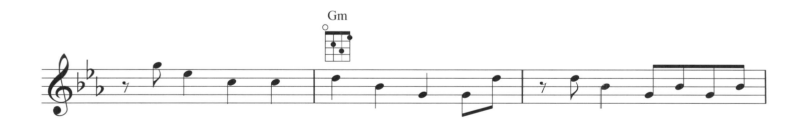

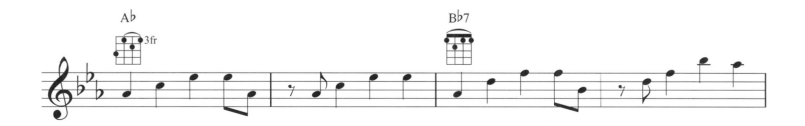

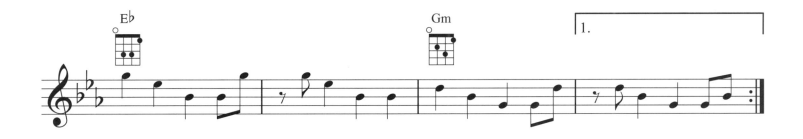

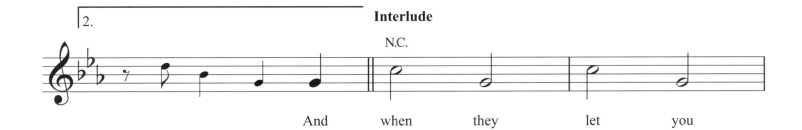

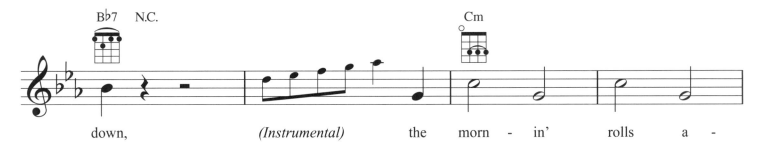

And   when   they   let   you

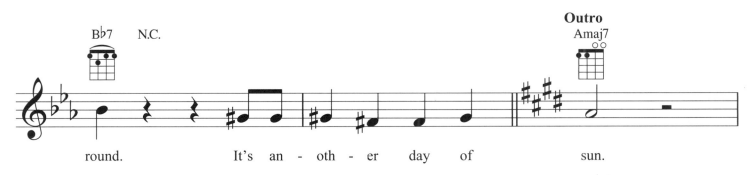

down,   *(Instrumental)*   the   morn - in'   rolls   a -

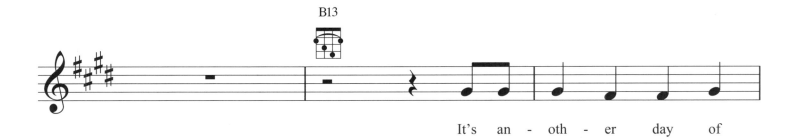

round.   It's an - oth - er   day   of   sun.

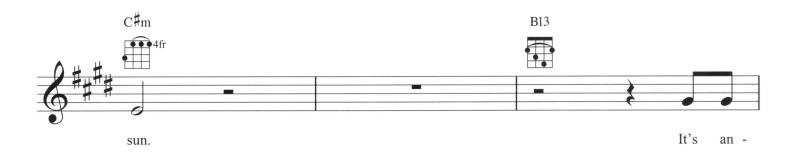

It's an - oth - er   day   of

sun.   It's an -

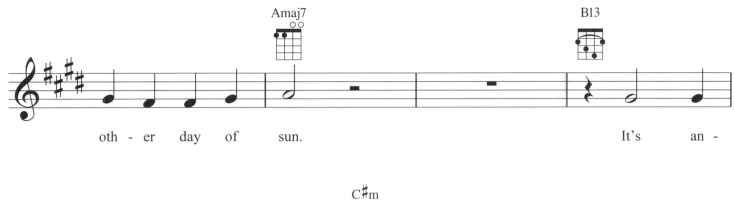

oth - er day of sun.

It's an -

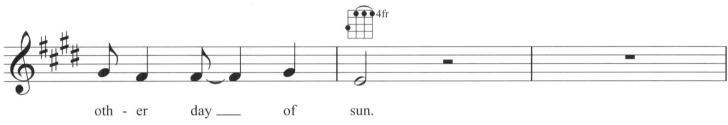

oth - er day ___ of sun.

Just an - oth - er day ___ of sun.

It's an - oth - er day of

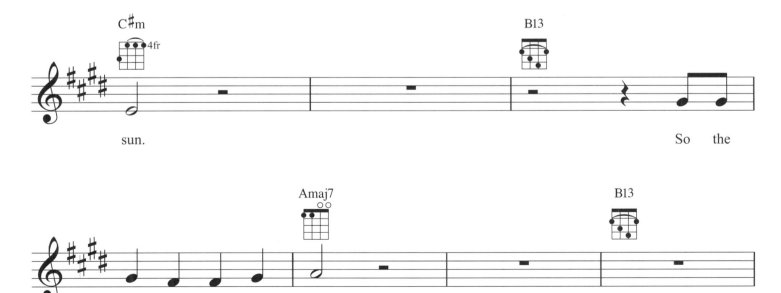

sun.

So the

day is just be - gun.

It's an - oth - er day of

Instrumental

sun. *(Vocal 1st time only)*

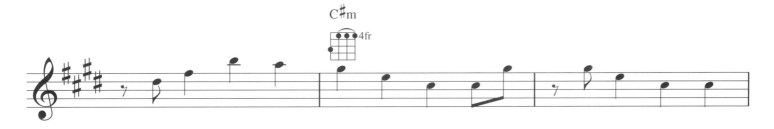

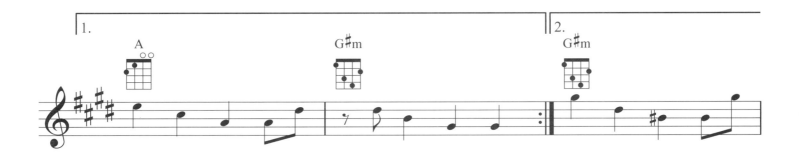

It's an -

oth - er day of sun. *(Instrumental)*

Audition
(The Fools Who Dream)

Music by Justin Hurwitz
Lyrics by Benj Pasek & Justin Paul

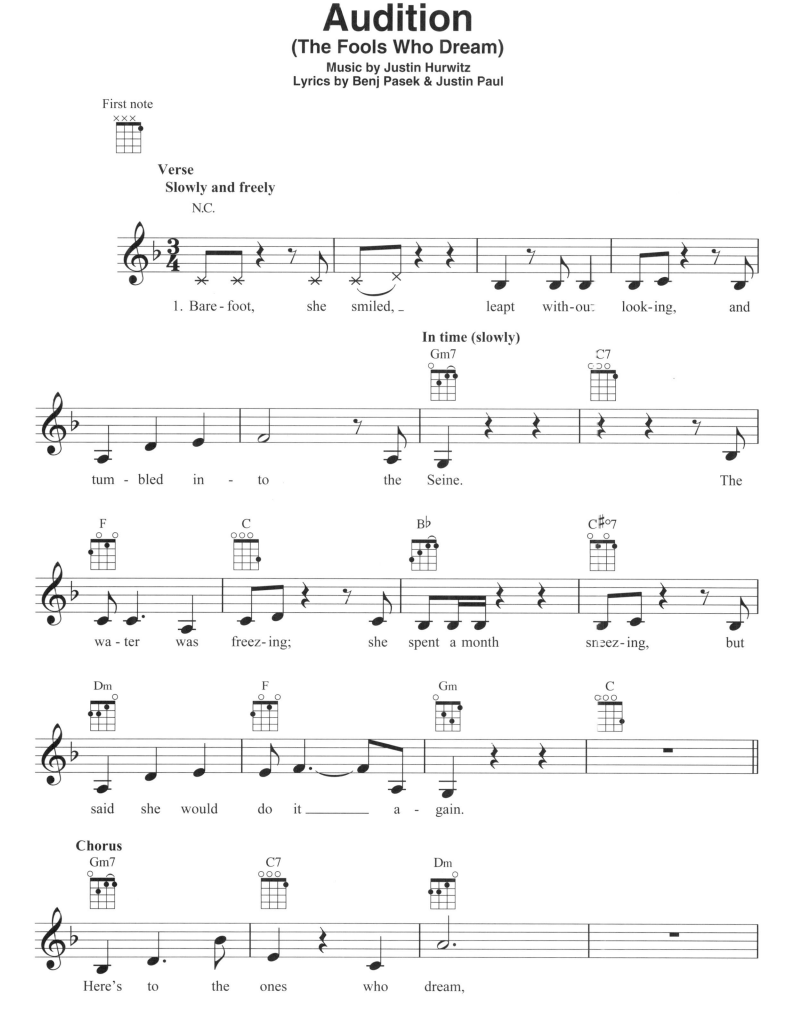

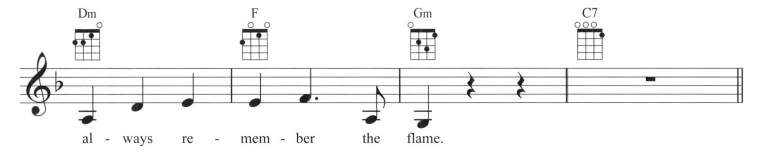

al - ways re - mem - ber the flame.

Chorus

Here's to the ones who dream,

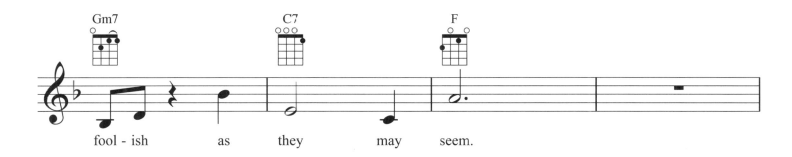

fool - ish as they may seem.

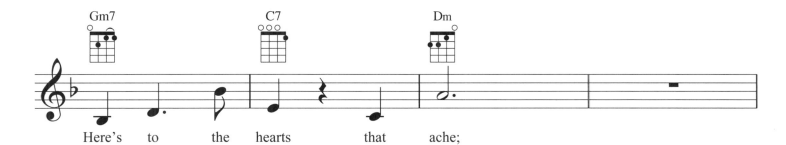

Here's to the hearts that ache;

here's to the mess we make. She

Bridge
Moderately

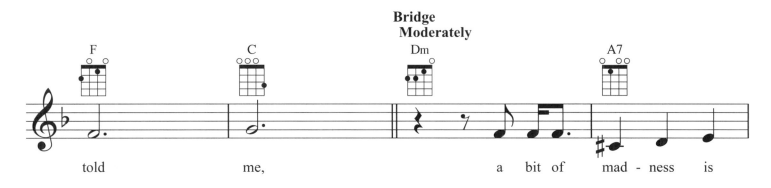

told me, a bit of mad - ness is

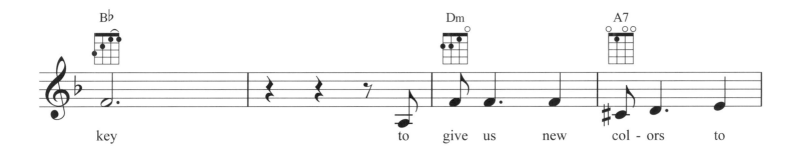

key _____ to give us new col - ors to

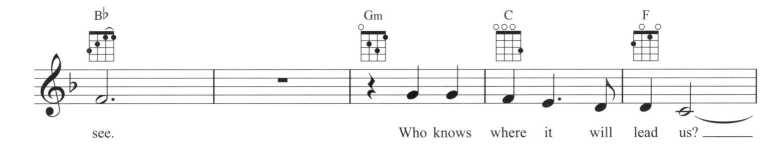

see. _____ Who knows where it will lead us? _____

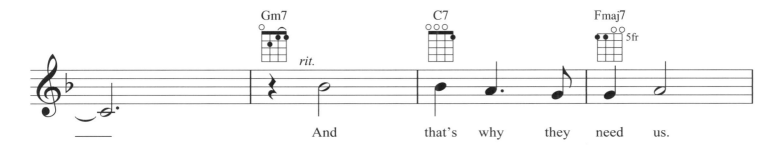

_____ And that's why they need us.

Broadening

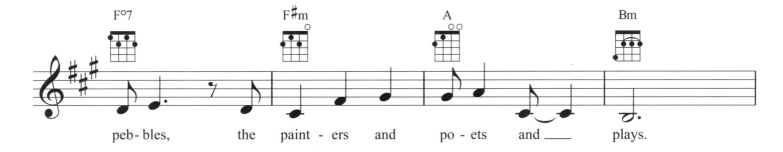

So, bring on _____ the reb - els, _____ the rip - ples from

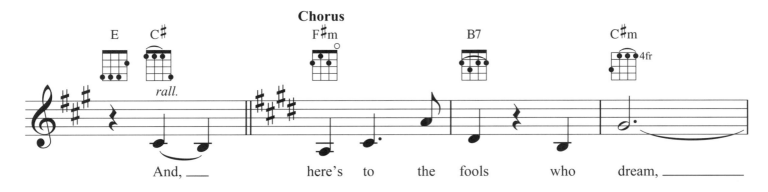

peb - bles, the paint - ers and po - ets and ___ plays.

Chorus

And, ___ here's to the fools who dream, _____

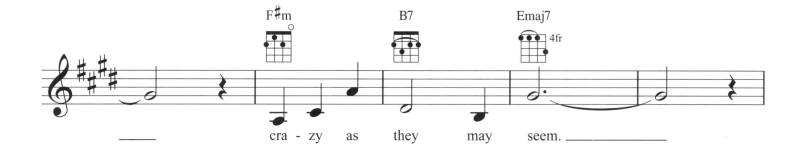

_____ cra - zy as they may seem. _____

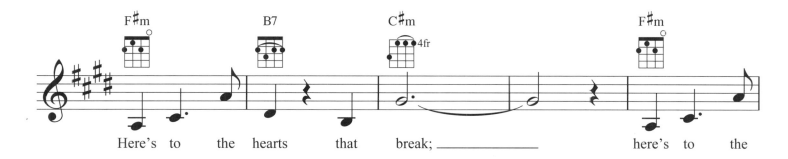

Here's to the hearts that break; _____ here's to the

Outro
Slower, with freedom

rit. e dim.

mess we make. I trace it

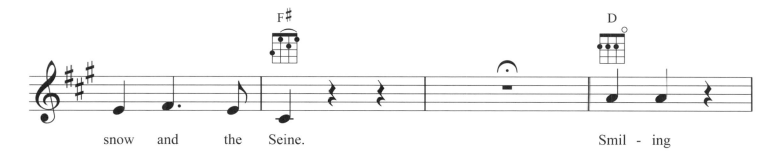

all back to then, her and the

snow and the Seine. Smil - ing

through it, she said she'd do it a - gain.

City of Stars

Music by Justin Hurwitz
Lyrics by Benj Pasek & Justin Paul

dreams may fi - n'lly come true.

Verse

2. Cit - y of stars, ___ just one thing ev - 'ry - bod - y wants,

there in the bars ___ and through the smoke-screen of the crowd - ed res - tau - rants: ___

it's love. Yes, all we're look - ing for is

love from some - one else. ___

Sebastian: A

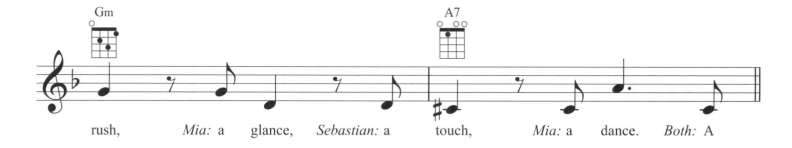

rush, *Mia:* a glance, *Sebastian:* a touch, *Mia:* a dance. *Both:* A

Bridge

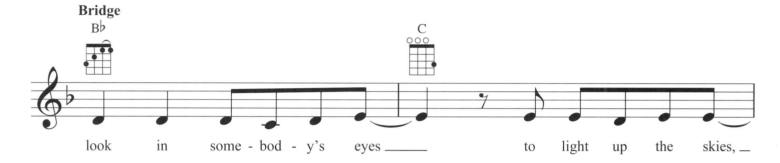

look in some - bod - y's eyes _____ to light up the skies, __

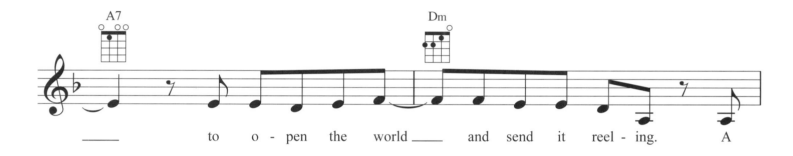

_____ to o - pen the world ____ and send it reel - ing. A

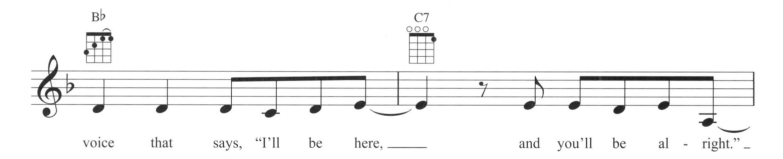

voice that says, "I'll be here, _____ and you'll be al - right." _

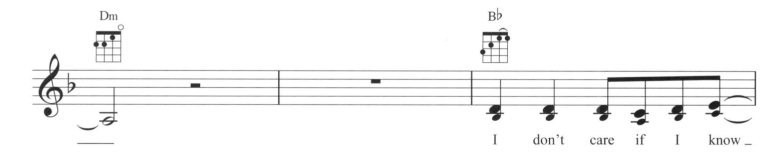

_____ I don't care if I know _

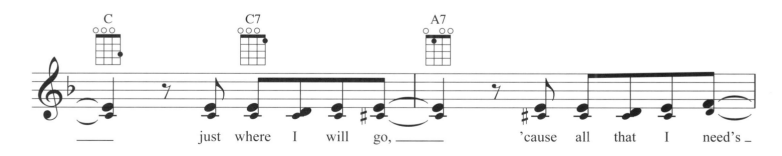

_____ just where I will go, _____ 'cause all that I need's _

____ this cra - zy feel - ing, a rat - tat - tat on my heart... ____

Freely

Sebastian: Think I want it to stay. ____

Outro-Verse

Cit - y of stars, ____

are you shin - ing just for me?

Slowly, freely

Cit - y of stars, ____ *Mia:* you nev - er shined so

bright - ly. ____

A Lovely Night

Music by Justin Hurwitz
Lyrics by Benj Pasek & Justin Paul

Chorus
Moderate Swing ($\sqcap$ = $\overset{3}{\sqcap}$)

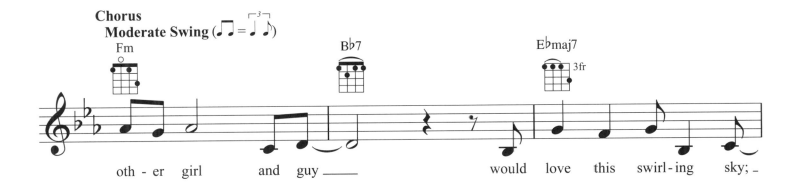

oth - er girl and guy _____ would love this swirl-ing sky; _

_____ but there's on - ly you and I, _____ and

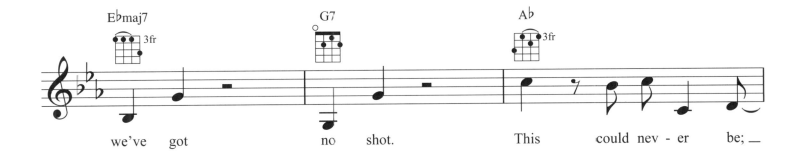

we've got no shot. This could nev - er be; _

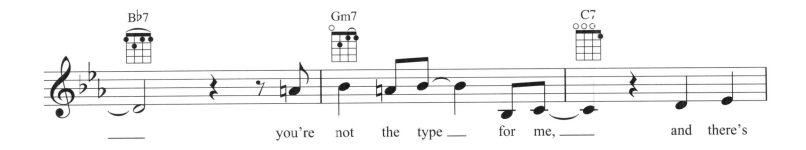

_____ you're not the type _____ for me, _____ and there's

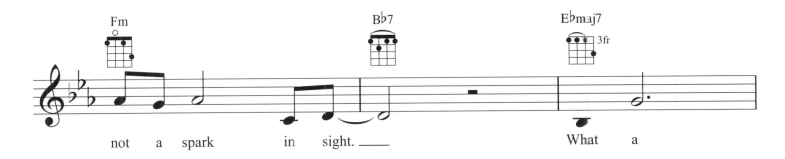

not a spark in sight. _____ What a

waste of a lov-e-ly night. _____

Verse
A bit faster

poco accel.

Mia: 2. You say there's noth-ing here; well,

let's make some-thing clear: I think I'll be the one __ to make that __

_____ call. And though you look so cute in your
Sebastian (spoken): But you'll call.

pol-y-es-ter suit, you're right: I'd nev-er fall for you at
It's wool.

Chorus

all. And may-be this ap-peals __

to some - one not in heels, ____ or to

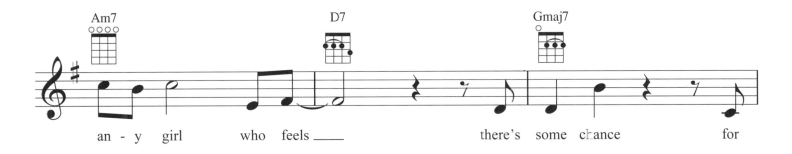

an - y girl who feels ____ there's some chance for

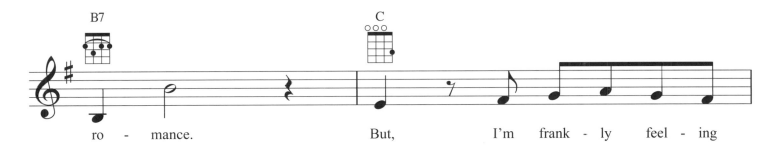

ro - mance. But, I'm frank - ly feel - ing

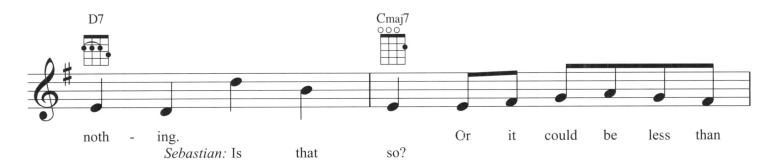

noth - ing.
Sebastian: Is that so? Or it could be less than

noth - ing.
Good to know! So you a - gree? That's right.

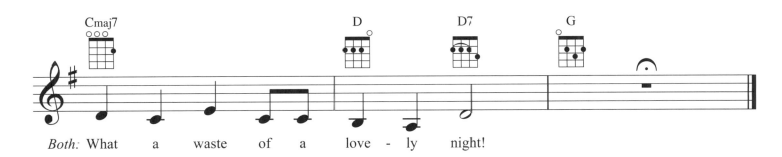

Both: What a waste of a love - ly night!

Someone in the Crowd

Music by Justin Hurwitz
Lyrics by Benj Pasek & Justin Paul

Verse

2. To - night we're on a mis - sion; to - night's the

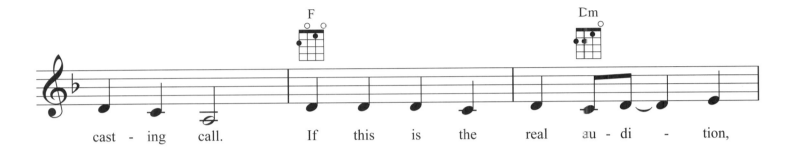

cast - ing call. If this is the real au - di - tion,

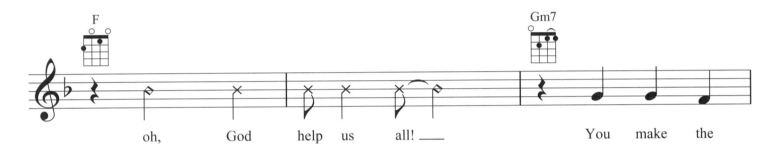

oh, God help us all! ___ You make the

right im - pres - sion, then ev - 'ry - bod - y knows your ___

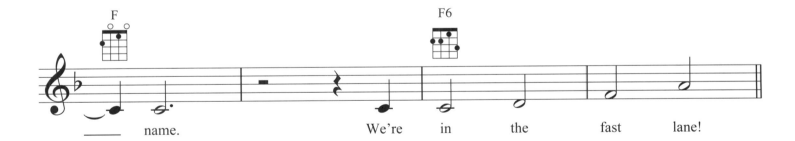

___ name. We're in the fast lane!

Chorus

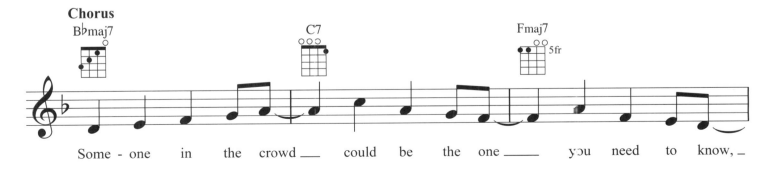

Some - one in the crowd ___ could be the one ___ you need to know, ___

the one to fi-n'lly lift you ___ off the

ground.   Some-one in the crowd _

___ could take you where you wan-na go, ___   if

you're the some-one read-y to be found,   the   some-one

read - y   to   be _____   found. _____
(Do   what   you   need   to ____ do

___   till   they   dis - cov - er ___   you,   and   make   you

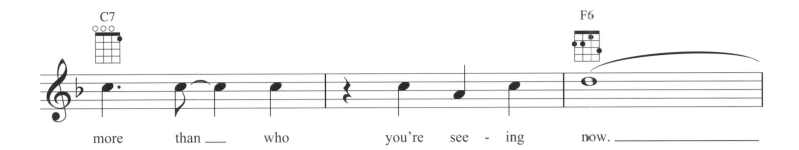

more than ___ who you're see - ing now. _____

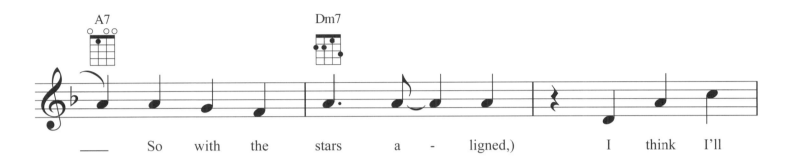

___ So with the stars a - ligned,) I think I'll

stay be - hind. (You've got to go and ___ find...) _

N.C.

_____ (Spoken): that

some - one in ___ the crowd. ___

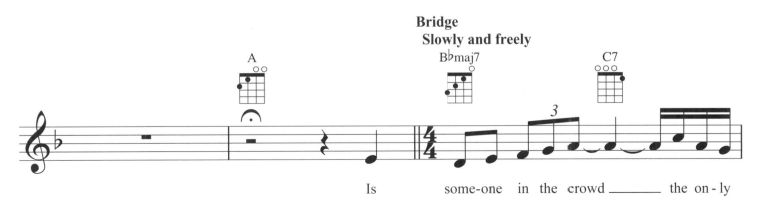

Bridge
Slowly and freely

Is some-one in the crowd _____ the on - ly

thing you ___ real-ly see, watch-ing while the world keeps spin-ning

'round? Some-where there's a place ___ where I ___ find

who I'm ___ gon-na be, a some-where that's just wait-ing to ___ be

Outro-Chorus
Tempo I

found. Some-one in the crowd ___ could be the one ___

___ you need to know, ___ the some-one who could lift ___

___ you ___ off the ground.

Some - one in the crowd ___ could take you where you wan - na go. ___

___ Some - one in the crowd ___ could make you,

some - one in the crowd ___ could take you fly - ing off the ground, ___

___ if you're the some - one read - y

to be found. _____

Start a Fire

Music & Lyrics by John Stephens, Angélique Cinélu, Marius De Vries and Justin Hurwitz

First note

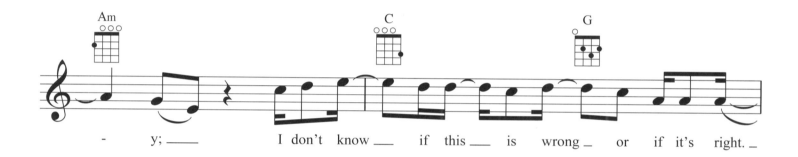

1. I don't know ___ why I keep ___ mov - in' ___ my bod -

- y; ___ I don't know ___ if this ___ is wrong ___ or if it's right. ___

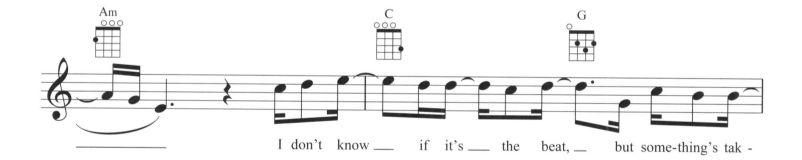

I don't know ___ if it's ___ the beat, ___ but some-thing's tak -

- ing o - ver me, ___ and I just know _ I feel ___ so good to-night. ___

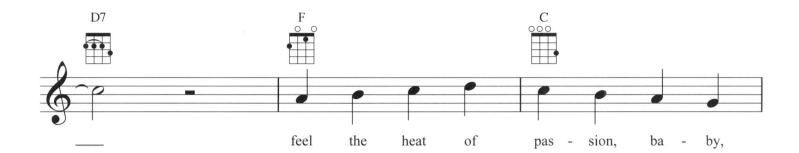

feel the heat of pas - sion, ba - by,

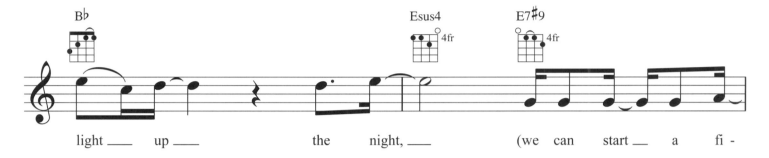

light ___ up ___ the night, ___ (we can start ___ a fi -

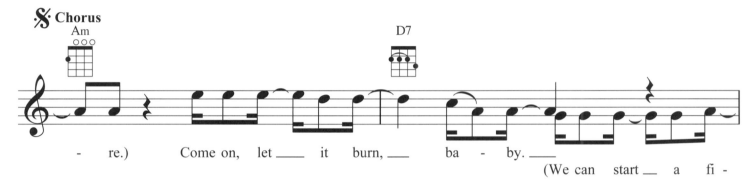

§ **Chorus**

- re.) Come on, let ___ it burn, ___ ba - by. ___ (We can start ___ a fi -

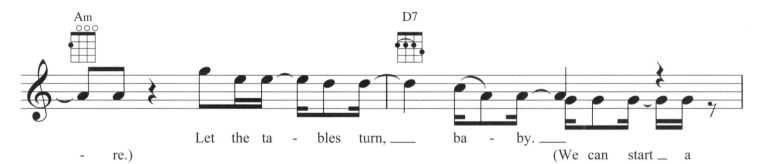

- re.) Let the ta - bles turn, ___ ba - by. ___ (We can start ___ a

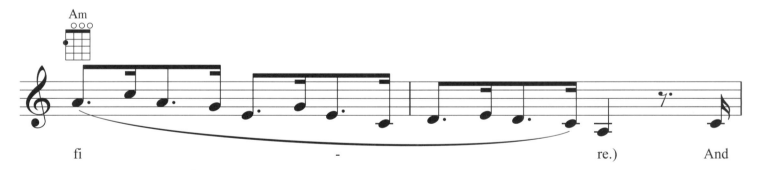

fi - re.) And

To Coda ⊕

I just know ___ I feel ___ so good, don't you know ___ I feel ___ so good,

I just know _ I feel _ so good _____ to - night. _

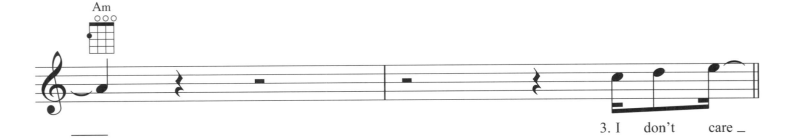

_____ 3. I don't care _

Verse

_____ if this turns _ in - to a ri - ot; _ let's get reck -

- less, tear _ this place _ down to the floor. _____ Turn the mu -

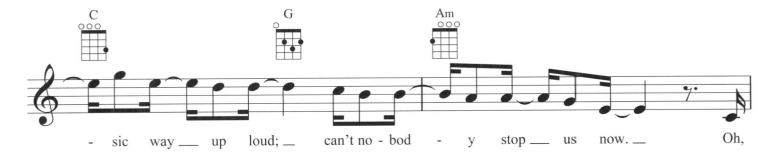

- sic way _ up loud; _ can't no - bod - y stop _ us now. _ Oh,

I just know _ I feel _ so good to - night. _ Oh, _____

Interlude

I just know __ I feel __ so good to-night. __

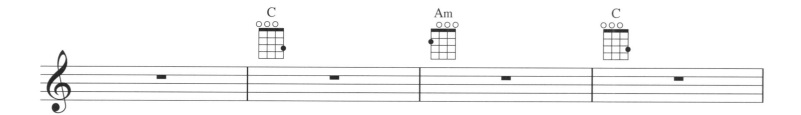

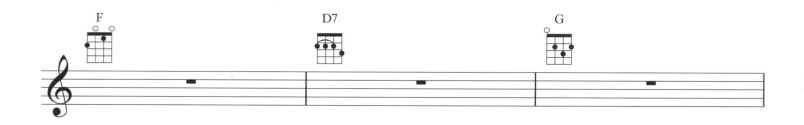

D.S. al Coda

(We can start __ a fi -

Coda

don't you know, __ don't you know, __

to - night. __